Displays and Interest Tables

Ready, Steady, Play!

Series Editor: Sandy Green

Guaranteed fun for children and practitioners alike, the Ready, Steady, Play! series provides lively and stimulating activities for children.

Each book focuses on one specific aspect of play offering clear and detailed guidance on how to plan and enjoy wonderful play experiences with minimum fuss and maximum success.

Each book in the Ready, Steady, Play! series includes advice on:

- How to prepare the children and the play space
- What equipment and materials are needed
- How much time is needed to prepare and carry out the activity
- How many staff are required
- How to communicate with parents and colleagues

Ready, Steady, Play! helps you to:

- Develop activities easily, using suggested guidelines
- Ensure that health and safety issues are taken into account
- Plan play that links to the early years curriculum
- Broaden your understanding of early years issues

Early years practitioners and students on early years courses and parents looking for simple, excellent ideas for creative play will love these books!

Other titles in the series

Books, Stories and Puppets 1-84312-148-4 Green
Construction 1-84312-098-4 Boyd
Creativity 1-84312-076-3 Green
Festivals 1-84312-101-8 Hewitson
Food and Cooking 1-84312-100-X Green
Music and Singing 1-84312-276-6 Durno
Nature, Living and Growing 1-84312-114-X Harper
Play Using Natural Materials 1-84312-099-2 Howe
Role Play 1-84312-147-6 Green

Displays and Interest Tables

Jayne Olpin

David Fulton Publishers

David Fulton Publishers Ltd
The Chiswick Centre, 414 Chiswick High Road, London W4 5TF

www.fultonpublishers.co.uk
www.onestopeducation.co.uk

First published in Great Britain in 2005 by David Fulton Publishers

10 9 8 7 6 5 4 3 2 1

Note: The right of Jayne Olpin to be identified as the author of this work has been
asserted by her in accordance with the Copyright, Designs and Patents Act 1988.

David Fulton Publishers is a division of Granada Learning Limited, part of ITV plc.

British Library Cataloguing in Publication Data
A catalogue record for this book is available from the British Library.

ISBN: 1 84312 267 7

Typeset by FiSH Books
Printed and bound in Great Britain

Contents

Displays and Interest Tables

Welcome to *Displays and Interest Tables*, an exciting new publication which is part of the Ready, Steady, Play! series.

Get ready to enjoy a range of activities with your children, which will stimulate their all-round development.

The Ready, Steady, Play! books will help boost the confidence of new practitioners by providing informative and fun ideas to support planning and preparation. The series will also consolidate and extend learning for the more experienced practitioner. Attention is drawn to health and safety, and the role of the adult is addressed.

How to use this book

Displays and Interest Tables is divided into four main sections.

Section 1 provides information on displays and interest tables and explains the forms of displays included in this book. It looks at some of the benefits to children through the process of producing displays. Health and safety issues and the role of the adult are also discussed.

Section 2 discussion pages are pages of displays that may be looked at with the children to encourage lots of discussion. It provides ideas for displays that the children can relate to.

Section 3 gives suggestions for displays, from simple table-top displays to more complex wall displays. This section will include instructions from preparing the boards through the process of enabling the children to produce the work, to mounting the work and putting the display together.

The fourth section provides photocopiable pages to support the displays throughout the book.

So read on, and enjoy ... **Ready, Steady, Play!**

Sandy Green
Series editor

Acknowledgements

Thank you to my husband Alan, daughter Amy and son Ben for their support and belief in me throughout the process of producing this book. Thanks to my daughter Amy, a BTec nursery nurse student, who designed the storyboard displays and worked with the children and staff in Little Learners nursery to produce them. A special thank you to Rachel, Ann and Lucy for their enduring encouragement throughout the process. They have always given me support, ideas and encouragement when needed.

A big thank you to all the children of Little Learners Nursery at Norton Radstock College for being so inspiring and willing to produce all of the displays in this book, and their parents for allowing the photographs to be used. The same thanks must go to all staff and students of Little Learners nursery for their co-operation.

A very special thank you to Sandy Green, the series editor, who has given me confidence in myself and endless support.

Series acknowledgement

The series editor would like to thank the children, parents and staff at:

- The Nursery and Reception class, Wadebridge County Primary School, Wadebridge, Cornwall
- Happy Days Day Nursery, Wadebridge, Cornwall
- Snapdragons Nursery, Weston, Bath, Somerset
- Snapdragons Nursery, Grosvenor, Bath, Somerset
- Tadpoles Nursery, Combe Down, Bath, Somerset

for allowing us to take photographs of their excellent provision, resources and displays.

Also to John and Jake Green, Jasmine and Eva for their help throughout the series, and to Nina, Margaret and Ben at David Fulton Publishers for their patience, enthusiasm and support.

Introduction

Displays are an important part of the work carried out in early years settings. They show children that their work is valued which in itself motivates them further and gives them a sense of pride in what they do both individually, and as part of a group. It also gives parents and carers an 'at a glance' opportunity to see what their child has been doing, enabling them to discuss it with the child.

Most displays have a focus, but it is important to remember that it is the children's ideas and interpretations which will make the end-product unique. The process is the important stage and the display is a celebration of the process. It is important that the children are allowed sufficient time to complete work to their satisfaction and planning should allow for this.

Practitioners are there to guide, support and encourage children to explore and experiment in their work and with their ideas for displays.

By discussing with children their ideas for displays we enable them to produce ideas and work that is unique to them and, through encouragement, practitioners must show that the children's work is valued. This will be achieved through praise, discussion, and by displaying the work appropriately, whether group work or individual efforts.

Displays come in many forms and may include:

- Interactive displays with lots of opportunities for exploration and experimentation.
- Wall displays of collections of work, remembering it is important to allow all children opportunities to take part.
- Wall displays of collections of individual work.
- Displays linked to topics – these may be ongoing throughout the period of the topic and added to during the topic, or may be a free-standing idea.
- Displays linked to children's stories in the form of one picture or a storyboard that shows different stages of the story.
- Displays for windows – double-sided for added interest.
- Table-top displays, closely linked with interactive displays. These may be downsized to tray displays for settings with limited space.

Producing displays offers a wide range of benefits, as the children are given opportunities to:

- Express themselves using their own ideas and thoughts.
- Explore and investigate.
- Consolidate and develop fine motor skills.
- Extend vocabulary both one-to-one with an adult or as part of a group through discussion and questioning.
- Develop social skills as they learn to work as part of a group, sharing and helping.
- Develop concentration skills as they focus on what they are producing.
- Gain emotional satisfaction regarding effort and achievement.

Health and safety

Good practice with regards to health and safety is very important when carrying out display work. Relevant points to consider include:

- Always maintain appropriate adult:child ratios.
- Ensure one-to-one or small groups for when closer supervision is needed (e.g. when using scissors and staplers).
- Be aware of any allergies children may have and provide alternatives.
- Ensure children are aware of and follow basic health and safety rules for the setting (e.g. hand-washing and safety with scissors).
- Be aware that many creative activities will produce 'mess' and therefore need to be carried out away from other activities, allowing less opportunities for distractions.
- All resources used need to be clean and non-toxic; craft items should be obtained from craft suppliers rather than through other means.
- Ensure hand-washing facilities are nearby when using paint, glue and so on to limit dripping of paint on the floors.
- All items used in displays need to be safe for the children to use and explore.

The adult role

As well as ensuring a healthy and safe environment for the children during preparation of display material, the adult has a number of other important roles, which include:

- Planning activities and displays carefully and providing sufficient and appropriate resources, ensuring an anti-discriminatory approach is taken.
- Ensuring children are involved in planning where appropriate, allowing them time to discuss their ideas for displays.
- Ensuring children have plenty of time to practise skills needed prior to the activity (e.g. practising with scissors if cutting skills are needed as part of the display work).
- Encouraging language development with appropriate discussion and open questioning.
- Ensuring praise and encouragement is given throughout preparation of display work, remembering that the children need the chance to explore through their work. An adult needs to intervene sensitively (i.e. only when needed).
- Observing children and assessing their progress.

One of the most vital decisions to be made is how much freedom of choice the children have with a display. It is so important that they have as much control as possible over their work that decisions should be made prior to the discussions with the children as to what is expected of them. For example, with storyboards, does the practitioner intend for the children to decide which sections of the story will be represented, or will the practitioner decide and allow the children to decide how these sections will be represented? This needs to be decided at the planning stage of the curriculum and may be determined by the learning outcomes you are aiming for.

Putting displays together

Interactive displays/table-top displays

These displays are exactly what they say they are: displays on tables or trays that the children are free to explore and investigate. Children have a natural curiosity which enables them to learn through exploring and playing. When putting these types of displays together health and safety must be the top priority. The children should be free to explore without fear of accidents, and for this reason all items within the display must be safe for all age ranges of children who will have access to them.

Interactive displays are often added to by the children bringing in items from home. When this is encouraged, parents/carers should be made aware of the health and safety issues. They also need to be made aware that all children will be handling the items; therefore it would be unfair to bring an item to the display that was very precious as it may be damaged, or the child whose item it is may be unable to cope with seeing it being handled by other children.

Interactive displays should look interesting and fun, and they should be set up in an area where the children can sit, either alone or in small groups, and explore in comfort without too many distractions. Adult interaction is great but should be not forced. Wait until they ask questions and encourage them to explore what is displayed. Present the items attractively but above all make them available.

Wall displays of group work

Make wall displays of collections of work, and displays that all children have made a contribution to, however small. Some children do not like to get 'messy' but love to use their writing skills; great for completing headings, or others may prefer printing activities; perhaps they could produce a border for the display. Other children may like to cut out pieces for the display. By using any of these skills all the children can be included in producing the display. It is not just about 'good art work'; it is also about allowing all children the opportunity to take part in the way they choose. The whole purpose of displays is to show what the children have produced to the best of their ability, not about the perfect piece of art work. All children's work is important.

When putting these displays together there are a number of things to think about:

- The colour of the background.
- The type of border.
- The arrangement of the display.

The colour of the background

This will depend on what the display is about, and often decides or limits the choice of colours. For the display on page 39 ('Under the sea'), blue seemed an obvious choice, whereas the display on page 47 ('Handprint picture') could have used any of the autumnal colours.

The type of border

Again, the content of the display will suggest the type of border. A contrasting colour is a good idea: black borders look striking on yellow or cream. A colour that complements the background colour also works well: dark blue on pale blue looks good. Sometimes it is nice to move away from the expected!

Use lots of handprints to frame a picture or encourage the children to print their own borders as shown on the opposite page.

The arrangement of the display

This may be determined by the content of the display. If you are following a pattern then obviously the order will be decided. The main points to remember are:

- to include the children in planning the 'putting together' of the displays as much as possible;
- to include work from all the children, as it is important that all children have a feeling of ownership of the display;
- to display children's work in the best way possible.

Groups of individual work

When displaying collections of children's individual work many of the above points are still valid. It is important not to bunch too many pictures/paintings together, and to allow space between the paintings. Sometimes more is less. Putting too many pictures in the display may detract from the quality of the pictures. Give them the space they deserve. If the child chooses to place their drawing in the top left part of a page rather than centrally, then that is how it should be displayed. It would be easy to cut the picture and make it central but that is not how the child intended it to be seen.

It is important to provide the children with well-cut pieces of paper, not a large sheet folded and torn roughly in half. Yes, it may be quicker, but every piece of a child's work is important and should be treated as such. When getting the pieces of art work ready for the wall display take the time to mount them carefully, leaving equal gaps around the edges of the piece of work. Some people prefer to leave a wider gap at the sides or at the top or bottom of the picture. Whichever you choose is fine, but it is important to make sure the picture is balanced.

Displays linked to topics

Displays linked to topics may be produced in one go or added to over the period of the topic. When displays are put together in this way it is an opportunity to give all children in the setting a sense of ownership. When displays are produced quickly they are often put together by children who come to the setting over a few days, and making them last longer gives all children an equal chance of being involved in some way, thus making the display a whole group effort.

Displays that are produced in this way sometimes have a natural pattern to follow. On the topic of weather you may choose to follow a different type of weather each week: wind, rain, snow, sun. In this way the display board will naturally fill over the course of the topic.

Displays linked to stories and rhymes

Children enjoy these displays as they are based on stories and rhymes they are familiar with. These types of displays can be in one of two forms: *either* a large picture as in the display on page 65 ('The wheels on the bus'), or in the form of a story as in the display on page 67 ('Patch bakes a cake'). Whichever form you choose to follow it is important to try to represent the story or rhyme in a style that the children can relate to. Let them choose which parts of the story or rhyme to represent, and give them a sense of ownership of the display whenever possible.

When the story follows a pattern you can *either* divide the board up into the number of sections required and use arrows or numbers to show the direction of the story ('Patch bakes a cake' is an example of this on pages 66–7), or allow the picture to flow, and again use arrows to indicate the direction needed to follow the pattern of the story.

Displays for windows

These displays have the added interest of natural light filtering through the window. This can add to the impact of the objects on display. Stained glass windows look spectacular with light coming through them. Another point to remember is that the objects on display may be seen from the outside as well, adding interest for the children when they arrive at the setting and for the parents to see also. These displays also give people outside an opportunity to see some of the creativity the children have produced. When thinking of ideas for these types of displays it is important to remember to try and make the items double-sided where possible (e.g. the display on page 73 'Snowy trees'). These trees looked stunning from outside as well as from inside, and the children loved to look at them when they were playing in the garden. Painting on the glass is another idea for decorating windows, it is a good idea to add a few drops of washing-up liquid to the paint before you paint, as this will help a great deal when you come to remove the paint from the window.

Which ever type of display you choose to do with the children in your setting the important thing to remember is that the children need to enjoy it. They need to have a sense of ownership of the display, and to be involved as much as possible.

Remember: A display is a celebration of the process the children have enjoyed and followed in order to produce it. The whole process should be fun and enjoyed by both children and adults, including students, staff and parents/carers.

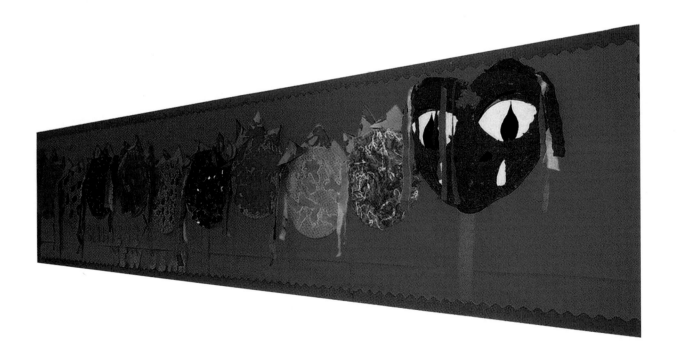

Discussion resources

The following section provides a range of photographs to stimulate discussion with children about or prior to creating a display, broadening their knowledge of presentation and encouraging thought, memory and description.

Have you played in the snow?

What can you see happening in this picture?

Do you know what this animals is?

Where might we find them?

What comes after autumn?

What is happening in this picture? How would you design a balloon?

What is this? What can you tell me about it?

Have you seen flowers like these?

Have you seen flowers like these?

What do you see?

What could we do with these?

Do you know what each of these is called?

What different patterns can you see?

How would these feel to touch?

What sort of display could we make on this background?

What sort of display could we make on this background?

What sort of display could we make on this background?

What sort of display could we make on this background?

Activities

The following pages contain 24 different activities using creative skills for display. Each activity follows a standard format to ensure ease of planning and implementation:

- the resources needed
- the aim(s)/concept(s)
- the process
- group size
- discussion ideas/language
- extension ideas
- links to the Foundation Stage Curriculum.

Key to Foundation Stage Curriculum abbreviations:

(SS)   Stepping stones

ELG   Early learning goals

PSE   Personal, social and emotional development

CLL   Communication, language and literacy

MD   Mathematical development

KUW   Knowledge and understanding of the world

PD   Physical development

CD   Creative development

ACTIVITY

1 Counting boxes

Resources you will need

- Ten boxes of different sizes
- Numbers 1 to 10
- Dots in groups of 1, 2, 3 . . . 10 drawn on paper
- Sellotape
- Buttons, compare bears or similar items to group into the boxes

Aim/concept

- To begin to experiment with numbers and counting

Process

- Discuss with the children the items you have collected.
- Look at the numbers 1 to 10. Count them with the children.
- Look at the groups of dots and encourage the children to match the dots to the numbers.
- Talk about the sizes of the boxes and comparing them.
- Explain to the children that they are going to stick the numbers on to the tops of the boxes and the dots to the same value on to the bottoms. When they have done this the children will place inside the boxes items of the same value (e.g. the number 4 on the top of the box, 4 dots on the bottom of the box and 4 buttons inside the box).
- Encourage the children to think about which boxes should be used for which number and allow them to experiment before you sellotape the numbers on to the boxes.
- When the boxes have been completed place them in the setting where they can be accessed easily by all the children.

Vocabulary/discussion

- Lots of language of numbers (e.g. bigger, smaller, more than, less than, numbers 1 to 10)
- Positional language (e.g. inside, outside, on top of, under, on the bottom).

Group size

Small groups or up to 10

Extension ideas

1. Link to topic of numbers and shapes.
2. Could be done with numbers up to 5.
3. Change numbers to letters of the alphabet.

Links to Foundation Stage Curriculum

PSE	Seek out others to share experiences (SS)
ELG	Work as part of a group or class, taking turns and sharing fairly, understanding that there need to be agreed values and codes of behaviour for groups of people, including adults and children, to work together harmoniously
CLL	Ask simple questions, often in the form of 'where' or 'what' (SS)
ELG	Interact with others, negotiating plans and activities and taking turns in conversation
MD	Show an interest in numbers and counting (SS)
ELG	Say and use number names in the correct order within familiar contexts
MD	Begin to represent numbers using fingers, marks on paper or pictures (SS)
ELG	Count reliably up to 10 everyday objects
ELG	Recognise numerals 1 to 9
ELG	Use developing mathematical ideas and methods to solve practical problems

ACTIVITY 2 Sound display

Resources you will need

- Child-sized table or tray for settings with limited space
- Child's illustrated dictionary
- Printed capital B and lower case b

Aim/concept

- To introduce the children to sounds, sound recognition

Process

- Gather the children into a group and talk about the sound that the letter A makes.
- Explain that they are going to put together a display of items from within the room that begin with the sound/letter A.
- Encourage them to practise making the sound. Look at the dictionary with them at the sound/letter A, discussing what they see. Can they name the items in the dictionary? Can they think of any other words or items that begin with the sound/letter A? Does their name begin with an A or is there an A in their name?
- Ask the children if they can think of items in the room that begin with the letter/sound A.
- When the children have come up with a number of items, encourage them to take it in turns to go and collect the items for the display.
- Discuss with the children the items they have collected.
- Encourage the children to decide how to display the items.

Vocabulary/discussion

- Talk about the sound the letter B makes
- Discuss the items the children have chosen

Group size

Whole group

Extension ideas

1. Make the sound display a weekly event – 'sound of the week'. Encourage the children to bring items from home to go on the display table/tray.
2. Whenever possible, use alliteration to emphasise the sound – if you cannot think of one for 'B', you could choose another letter as an example.

Links to Foundation Stage Curriculum

PSE Relate and make attachments to members of the group (SS)

ELG Work as part of a group or class, taking turns and sharing fairly, understanding that there need to be agreed values and codes of behaviour for groups of people, including adults and children, to work together harmoniously

CLL Respond to simple instructions (SS)

ELG Sustain attentive listening, responding to what they have heard by relevant comments, questions or actions

CLL Distinguish one sound from another (SS)

ELG Link sounds to letters, naming and articulating the letters of the alphabet

ACTIVITY
3 Colour display

Resources you will need

- Child-sized table or tray for settings with limited space
- Green cloth or large piece of paper to cover surface
- Written label 'Green'
- Book of colours

Aim/concept

- To introduce the children to colours, colour recognition, taking turns

Process

- Look at the colour book with the children.
- Discuss the chosen colour – green.
- What can they think of that is green?
- Explain to the children that they are going to produce a 'green display' using items from the setting.
- Let the children cut the fabric or paper for the display area and set it out.
- Encourage the children to collect items from within the room for the display.
- Discuss the chosen items with the children, noting the different shades of green and textures of the items.
- Encourage the children to decide how to display the items.

Vocabulary/discussion

- Talk about different shades of green.
- Discuss textures of the chosen items.

Group size

6–8

Extension ideas

1. Make the colour display a weekly event – 'colour of the week'. Encourage the children to bring items from home to go on the display table/tray.
2. Take the children on a 'colour walk', looking for the chosen colours in the natural enviroment surrounding the setting.
3. Produce an activity sheet containing green items from within the setting and encourage the children to colour them in when found.
4. Make green paint with the children using yellow and blue.
5. Help the children change the colour of playdough by adding green food dye.

Links to Foundation Stage Curriculum

KUW Describe simple features of objects and events (SS)

ELG Investigate objects and materials by using all their senses as appropriate

CD Begin to differentiate colours (SS)

ELG Explore colour, texture, shape, form and space in two or three dimensions

ACTIVITY 4 Investigation bottles

Resources you will need

- Water
- Plastic jug
- Pipette
- Funnel
- Cooking oil
- Glitter
- Plastic bottles of various sizes
- Food colouring of various colours
- Washing up liquid
- Sand
- Rice
- Dried peas
- Sellotape

Aim/concept

- To experiment with different items in the bottles and their effect

Process

- Gather the items together and place them on the table. Discuss them with the children. Talk about the colours and textures of the items.
- Explain that the items are going to be placed in the bottles and talk about what they think might happen, what the effects might be.
- Explain that some of the bottles will have water in them and others will not. Then they will be able to see what happens when the bottles are shaken.
- Encourage the children to fill some of the bottles with water using the funnel and jug, leaving a gap at the top of the bottle so that it is three-quarters full.
- Using the pipette, drop food colouring into the bottle, a different bottle for each colour. Replace the lid and fix firmly with Sellotape.
- Encourage the children to shake the bottle and watch and discuss the results.
- Repeat the last step with the washing up liquid, cooking oil and glitter.
- With the remaining bottles use the funnel to place the sand, rice and dried peas into separate bottles, this time placing enough of the substance to make a noise, and see what effect they have. Make sure the lids are firmly fixed with Sellotape. Again, talk to the children about the various noises the different items make.
- When the bottles are complete bring all of the children together as a group, and explore and discuss the bottles together.
- Place the bottles on a table where the children can explore them on their own or in groups as an interactive display.

Vocabulary/discussion

- Discuss the process as it takes place introducing new language where possible (e.g. pouring, into, shakes, mix).
- Talk about the noises; are they soft or loud?
- Compare the peas and rice: which one is heavier?
- Look at the bottles: which are bigger and which are smaller?

Group size

Whole group to discuss, break into small groups to complete activity, then back to the whole group to discuss and explore

Extension ideas

1. Encourage weighing activities, making comparisons and predictions.
2. Use peas, rice, sand and so on for collage work or simply to handle (in small bowls).

Links to Foundation Stage Curriculum

PSE Show curiosity (SS)

ELG Continue to be interested, excited and motivated to learn

CLL Talk activities through, reflecting on and modifying what they are doing (SS)

ELG Use talk to organise, sequence and clarify thinking, ideas, feelings and events

MD Order two items by weight or capacity (SS)

ELG Use language such as 'greater', 'smaller', 'heavier' or 'lighter' to compare quantities

KUW Show curiosity and interest by facial expression, movement or sound (SS)

ELG Investigate objects and materials by using all their senses as appropriate

ACTIVITY 5

Rhyme boards

Resources you will need

- Large pieces of card
- Typed words of the rhyme
- Photocopies of the pictures from books or hand-drawn pictures to match the rhyme
- Velcro
- Glue stick

Aim/concept

- To use the finished boards and explore the rhyme independently with confidence

Process

- Choose from a list of their favourite familiar rhymes:

    Five fat sausages sizzling in a pan
    Five cheeky monkeys jumping on the bed
    Five currant buns in a baker's shop
    and so on.

- Talk to the children about the rhyme.
- Explain to the children that they are going to place the words for the rhyme and pictures on to a board so that they can move pieces around on the board as they sing the rhyme.
- Encourage the children to cut out the words for the rhyme and place them on the board using a glue stick.
- Choose some pictures to use for the rhyme or draw some pictures with the children (e.g. five currant buns and a shop window, and a plate to put the buns on when they have been bought).
- Encourage the children to cut out the pictures ready to go on to the board.
- If possible, laminate the pictures that will be moved (e.g. the buns). If not, use strong card to draw the pictures on. You may need to cut out the pictures yourself if card is used.
- Attach a small piece of Velcro to the back of the buns and also to the places on the board where the buns will be (e.g. in the shop window and on the plate).
- Encourage the children to sing the rhyme when it is complete and take it in turns to move the pieces around the board.
- When the activity is complete place the boards on the wall and encourage the children to use them either by themselves or in small groups.

Vocabulary/discussion

- Encourage the children to think about the rhyme they are using and repeat the words of the rhyme.
- Talk about the actions in the rhyme. Have they been to a shop and bought cakes? Have they cooked sausages with their parents? Did they sizzle or pop?

Group size

4–6

Links to Foundation Stage Curriculum

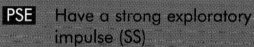

PSE	Have a strong exploratory impulse (SS)
ELG	Continue to be interested, excited and motivated to learn
CLL	Listen to favourite nursery rhymes, stories and songs, and join in with repeated refrains, anticipating key events and important phrases (SS)
ELG	Enjoy listening to and using spoken and written language, and readily turn to it in play and learning
MD	Enjoy joining in with number rhymes and songs (SS)
ELG	Say and use number names in the correct order within familiar contexts
CD	Join in favourite songs (SS)
ELG	Recognise and explore how sounds can be changed, sing simple songs from memory, recognise repeated sounds and sound patterns, and match movement to music

Extension ideas

1. Put numbers on the sausages/cakes and encourage number recognition.
2. Use the same ideas for stories and make props for the story. Encourage the children to tell the story using their pictures as props.

ACTIVITY 6 Under the sea

Resources you will need

- Pictures of under the sea and creatures who live there
- Pre-cut fish shapes, crabs and sea-horses or shapes for the children to cut out
- Various types of brightly coloured paper and card
- Odds and ends of fabric and shiny materials
- Small pots of PVA glue and spatulas
- Small pots of lentils and pasta
- Shallow trays of paint
- Scissors
- Aprons
- Sequins
- Egg boxes

Aim/concept

- To explore fabric, paint and materials to create a picture

Process

- Talk to the children about what lives under the sea.
- Show them pictures of fishes, sea-horses and crabs.
- Discuss the colours of the creatures and the plant life.
- Explain to the children that they are going to make an 'under the sea' display.
- Support the children in cutting out their own fishes or provide pre-cut shapes for those who need them.
- Examine all the materials available to the children and talk about what they would like to use, discussing the textures and colours of the chosen items.
- Encourage the children to work alone or in pairs to decorate the fishes, crabs and sea-horses.
- Use one section of an egg box for eyes that stand out if desired by the child. Provide examples that they might 'choose' from.
- Discuss the seaweed with the children and encourage them to use their handprints to re-create the seaweed as a backdrop for the under the sea display.
- Discuss with the children where they would like their creatures to go on the display, encouraging them to plan/own the display.
- Cut out the letters for the heading and encourage the children to colour them in.

Vocabulary/discussion

- Discuss life under the sea, creatures and colours
- Talk about the materials available and their texture and colour (e.g. shiny, smooth, rough, bright)

Group size

Pairs or small groups of 3–4

Extension ideas

1. Link to general topic of 'Water' or 'Under the sea'.
2. Discuss with the children their experiences of water/sea on holidays; did they see any fish in the water?
3. Talk to the children about pets. Do any of them have pet fish, or have they seen tropical fish in fish tanks?
4. Discuss fish with the children, explaining that some fish live in warm water and some in cold water.

Links to Foundation Stage Curriculum

PSE Show confidence in linking up with others for support and guidance (SS)

ELG Be confident to try new activities, initiate ideas and speak in a familiar group

CD Show an interest in what they see, hear, smell, touch and feel (SS)

ELG Respond in a variety of ways to what they see, hear, smell, touch and feel

Health and safety

⚠ Explain that the lentils and pasta provided are not for eating
⚠ Careful supervision of scissor use
⚠ Non-toxic glues
⚠ Careful supervision of younger children with small items

7 Group mural

Resources you will need

- Aprons
- Rolls of lining paper
- Shallow containers of paint
- Paintbrushes
- Paint rollers
- Sponges
- Bubble wrap – scrunched up and sealed with an elastic band
- Scrapers
- Cotton reels
- Hands and fingers!

Aim/concept

- For children to explore paint and colour

Process

- Explain to the children that the activity involves using all resources available and seeing what effect they have.
- Talk to the children about the various utensils available to them, what patterns do they think they might produce?
- Allow the children to experiment with the utensils and paint.
- Talk to the children about the patterns and effects the utensils produce. Encourage them to use description.
- Encourage the children to share the utensils and choice of colours of paint, working co-operatively.
- Display the group effort.

Vocabulary/discussion

- Names of utensils available and their 'normal' uses
- Names of colours used
- Introduce new descriptive words (e.g. dab, spread, pat)
- Introduce comparative language (e.g. the same as, similar, compare)

Group size

4–6

Extension ideas

1. Link to a general topic on colours and shapes, patterns.
2. Create individual paintings for each of the utensils and encourage the children to make comparisons between them.
3. Design wrapping paper and use to wrap up boxes.

Links to Foundation Stage Curriculum

KUW	Explore objects (SS)
ELG	Look closely at similarities, differences, patterns and change
PD	Use one-handed tools and equipment (SS)
ELG	Handle tools, objects, construction and malleable materials safely and with increasing control
CD	Use their bodies to explore texture and space (SS)
ELG	Explore colour, texture, shape, form and space in two or three dimensions

ACTIVITY 8 Daffodils, butterflies and caterpillars

Resources you will need

- Green sugar paper
- White paper
- Green card
- Red card
- Shallow trays of various colours of paint
- Cardboard egg boxes
- Scissors
- Pencils
- Daffodils
- Wall stapler

Aim/concept

- To develop and extend fine motor and manipulative skills

Process

- Look at the daffodils with the children, and discuss the colour and shapes of the petals, stems and leaves.
- Discuss insects they may have seen in the garden around the flowers.
- Talk to the children about the display they are going to produce listening to and encouraging their ideas.
- Demonstrate to the children the petal shape required to produce the flowers and encourage and support them to draw and cut out the petal shapes.
- Once the shapes are ready they can be painted.
- Look at the stems and leaves of the flowers and encourage and support the children to cut them out.
- The caterpillars may be made from strips of card folded concertina-style. This can be demonstrated to the children before supporting their efforts.
- Encourage the children to cut out the butterflies and paint them in colours of their choice. By folding them over the colours will mix beautifully.
- The centres of the daffodils may be made from egg boxes painted to match the petals.
- Discuss with the children how they want their picture to look and where they want to put their flowers and insects, and assemble it with them. Ensure an adult has total control of the stapler.

Vocabulary/discussion

- Talk to the children about the various parts of a flower – stem, petals, leaves
- Discuss butterflies and caterpillars
- Talk about colour and symmetry

Group size
4

Extension ideas

1. Link to topics on growing.
2. Produce an activity sheet on various parts of a flower.
3. Place the daffodils in water with food colouring and watch them change colour

Links to Foundation Stage Curriculum

PSE Have a positive approach to new ideas (SS)

ELG Continue to be interested, excited and motivated to learn

CLL Use simple statements and questions often linked to gestures (SS)

ELG Interact with others, negotiating plans and activities and taking turns in conversation

KUW Show curiosity, observe and manipulate objects (SS)

ELG Investigate objects and materials by using all of their senses as appropriate

ACTIVITY 9 Flowers display

Resources you will need

- Aprons
- Diffusing paper
- Water
- Green sugar paper
- Scissors
- Felt pens

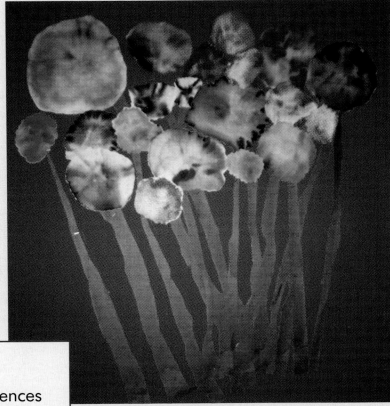

Aim/concept

- To enjoy new experiences

Process

- Talk to the children about the activity and what they are going to do.
- Explain to the children that the flowers they make will form a display.
- Encourage the children to cut their own 'stems' for their flowers, helping them if necessary.
- Encourage the children to draw circles or flower shapes using diffusing paper, supporting them if necessary.
- Make the flower shapes wet and watch the colours 'grow'.
- Discuss the effect the water has on the paper, encouraging the children to articulate what they see and introduce new words as appropriate.
- When the flowers have dried, encourage and support the children to cut them out.
- Discuss with the children where they would like their flowers to go on the display and how the display will be put together.

Vocabulary/discussion

- Encourage the children to discuss the changes in the flowers as the colour starts to diffuse
- Use vocabulary (e.g. spreading, darker, lighter, blend, merge, mix) to describe the colours

Group size

4–6

Extension ideas

1. Link to topic of colour.
2. Link to a topic on changes.

Links to Foundation Stage Curriculum

PSE	Have a positive approach to new experiences (SS)
ELG	Continue to be interested, excited and motivated to learn
MD	Observe and use positional language (SS)
ELG	Use everyday words to describe position
KUW	Talk about what is seen and what is happening (SS)
ELG	Ask questions about why things happen and how things work
CD	Work creatively on a large or small scale (SS)
ELG	Explore colour, texture, shape, form and space in two or three dimensions

ACTIVITY 10 Handprint picture

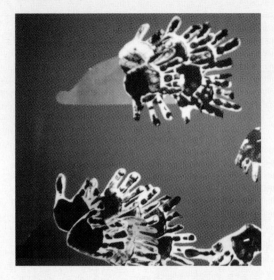

Resources you will need

- Natural autumn leaves
- Aprons
- White paper
- Brushes
- Twigs
- Brown sugar paper
- Pots of PVA glue
- Glue spreaders
- Child-sized scissors
- Photos of autumn trees and hedgehogs
- Shallow trays of various autumn-coloured paints
- Scraps of brown material and paper
- Staple gun
- Hands!

Aim/concept

- To explore autumn colours in paint

Process

- Look at the autumn photos and/or leaves. Has anyone seen trees like this in these colours?
- Discuss the colours: which do they like? Talk about the shades.
- Explain to the children that they are going to produce lots of leaves by painting their hands with the autumn-coloured paints.
- Encourage the children to paint their hands and then print lots of hands on paper.
- Explain that they will need lots of brown prints to produce the hedgehogs.
- Let the children draw the trunk of the tree and cut it out for the display.
- Provide the children with the choices of scraps of material and paper to decorate the trunk of the tree.
- Encourage the children to draw the hedgehog shape or provide pre-cut shapes.
- When all pieces of the display have dried and been cut out talk to the children about how they want to put the display together.
- Start with the trunk and fix to the display with staple gun.
- The twigs will need to be glued into place.
- Let the children assemble the hedgehogs on a table, then transfer to the display board.
- Talk to the children about falling leaves and suggest that some of their prints could be falling.

Vocabulary/discussion

- Talk about the season of autumn, the shades of the colours, the textures of the leaves.
- Talk about the parts of the tree (e.g. trunk, branches and leaves).
- Look at the leaves and discuss the similarities and textures.

Group size

Pairs or small groups

Extension ideas

1. Link to topic of weather.
2. Link to topic of changes.
3. Go on a nature walk and look closely at the surroundings.
4. Collect a variety of leaves and look at similarities and differences. Show pictures of the different trees and match the leaves to the trees.

Links to Foundation Stage Curriculum

PSE Show curiosity (SS)

ELG Continue to be interested, excited and motivated to learn

KUW Show an interest in the world in which they live (SS)

ELG Observe, find out about and identify features in the place they live and the natural world

ACTIVITY 11 Snowmen

Resources you will need

- Scissors
- Dark blue paper
- Green paper
- Black paper
- Orange paper
- White card
- White paint
- Brown paint
- Green paint
- Sponge square for printing
- Fingers for printing
- PVA glue
- Cotton wool
- Hole punch

Aim/concept

- To make choices and use the imagination

Process

- Talk to the children about their experiences of snow. Have they played in the snow, built snowmen? Talk to the children about the display they are going to make, describe the trees and snowmen and explain how they are going to make them. Talk about the snowflakes and that they are going to 'walk' their fingers over the paper to make the snowflakes.
- Lay the blue paper on the floor or table and encourage the children to place their fingers in the white paint and then make snowflakes on the paper by 'walking' their fingers over the paper.
- Dip the sponge into the white paint and stamp the sponge over the green paper to make the ground, the lower part of the display.
- Place these two pieces of the display on the wall once they have dried.
- Using the white card, encourage the children to draw around their hands and then cut them out. Give encouragement and offer assistance if needed. Some of the hands will need to be painted green and some brown to create the trees in the picture.
- To make the snowmen the children should be encouraged to draw and cut out two circles. These can be placed together and then glued and covered in cotton wool. By using a hole punch on black paper this will create perfect-sized eyes for the snowmen. Just add an orange triangle to complete the snowmen's features. The hats and boots are cut from black paper. The children may draw and cut them out or some may need them cut out for them. When putting the snowmen together the children should be given complete control in making decisions as to what goes where. From the results of this display you can see that this makes the picture unique.
- Give the children the opportunity to plan the picture from this point. Let them decide where their snowman will be placed and the same for the trees.
- Finish off the display by using a white border.

Vocabulary/discussion

- Talk to the children about their experiences of snow.
- Encourage them to share their experiences. Have they felt the snow? Was it cold? Have they built snowmen or snowballs? What did they use to decorate their snowman? What clothes did they wear when they played in the snow? Did they get wet?
- Lots of discussion about their experiences of snow.

Group size

Whole group to plan and discuss and then in pairs or small groups

Extension ideas

1. Link to a topic of weather.
2. Link to a topic of winter.
3. Collect a variety of items of clothing for various weathers and four boxes with weather symbols on the front (sun, snow, wind and rain). Encourage the children to think about which clothes they would choose for which weather.
4. Look at ice in detail. Fill a rubber glove with water and freeze, and when frozen remove the glove and drop food colouring on to the ice and watch!

Links to Foundation Stage Curriculum

KUW Display high levels of involvement in activities (SS)

ELG Be confident to try new activities, initiate ideas and speak in a familiar group

MD Observe and use positional language (SS)

ELG Use everyday words to describe position

CD Further explore an experience using a range of senses (SS)

ELG Respond in a variety of ways to what they see, hear, smell, touch and feel

ACTIVITY
12 Spring

Resources you will need

- Blue paper
- Green paper
- White paper
- Cream card for tree
- Scissors
- Sand
- Card for hand daffodils
- Card for small flowers
- Cardboard egg boxes
- Pencils
- Tissue paper in various colours
- Pictures of spring flowers or bunch of daffodils

- Yellow paint
- Orange paint
- Brown paint
- Green paint

Aim/concept

- To create a representation of 'spring' using the imagination

Process

- Talk to the children about the spring pictures or the flowers. Encourage them to share their experiences of spring. Have they seen any daffodils in their gardens or grown them? Have they seen buds on the trees? If possible, take the children on a nature walk prior to the discussion.
- Explain to the children that they are going to make a tree for the display board. Encourage them to draw and cut out the different parts of the tree (e.g. the trunk and branches). When these have been cut out talk to the children about the paint they will be using to decorate the tree, namely paint mixed with sand. Ask them how they think the paint will feel when it has dried: rough or smooth?
- To make the daffodil flowers, encourage the children to draw around their hands. They will need four hand prints to make a daffodil. When the hands have been cut out they will need to be painted yellow. Talk to the children about the colours of the flowers. By painting the egg box section orange this will form the centre of the flower. Encourage the children to cut out stalks for their flowers and arrange them together when the paint has dried.
- The small flowers are formed by encouraging the children to draw and cut out the flower shapes. The flowers can be decorated by screwing up small pieces of tissue paper and sticking these to the flowers.
- Talk to the children about where they would like to place their flowers on the display board. Encourage them to talk about the various textures involved in the display.
- The border in this display was produced by providing the children with strips of white paper and encouraging them to 'stamp' shapes over the border paper.

Vocabulary/discussion

- Talk to the children about spring (e.g. the flowers, buds, lambs, parts of the tree and flowers, trunk, branches, stems and leaves).
- Discuss the colours used and the name of the flowers.
- Talk about the textures involved in the display (e.g. rough and smooth).

Group size

Whole group to discuss the project and then one-to-one or small groups

Links to Foundation Stage Curriculum

PSE Show curiosity (SS)
ELG Maintain attention, concentrate, and sit quietly when appropriate
CLL Have emerging self-confidence to speak to others abouts wants and interests (SS)
ELG Interact with others, negotiating plans and activities and taking turns in conversation
CD Begin to differentiate colours (SS)
ELG Explore colour, texture, shape, form and space in two or three dimensions

Extension ideas

1. Link to topic on seasons.
2. Link to topic on growing.
3. Plant seeds and watch them grow or place bulbs over water to see them sprout and grow.

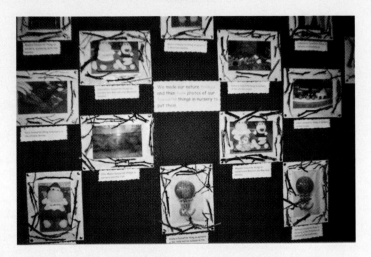

ACTIVITY
13 Favourite things

Resources you will need

- White card
- Craft knife
- Twigs
- PVA glue
- Camera (digital or 35m), or pictures of equipment to cut out
- Child-sized scissors

Aim/concept

- For children to make choices and produce their own photo frame

Process

- Talk to the children about the items in the setting. Encourage them to choose their favourite.
- Give the children the camera and help them take photos of their chosen item in the setting or to cut out pictures from magazines of their favourite things.
- If a digital camera is used the children can help print their photos on the computer if there is one in the setting.
- If a 35m camera is used, talk to the children about how the film has to go to be developed. Ask them if they have taken films to be developed before.
- Show the children the developed film. Support them in identifying which photograph they each took.
- Cut the card, with the craft knife, so that it is larger than the size of the photo and then cut an opening a little smaller than the photo, with a border of at least 5cm.
- Encourage the children to decorate the frames with the twigs, measuring them as they go.
- When the twigs are glued into place make sure the children cover the twigs with glue to seal them and make them shine.
- When dry, place the frame over the photo and fix into place.
- Cut out a piece of card for the backing and fix with glue.
- Place the photos on the display board.

Vocabulary/discussion

- Talk to the children about things they like and why they like them
- Encourage them to discuss their choices with the group

Group size

Whole group for discussion, then in pairs or small groups for assembling the frames

Kai's favourite thing in nursery is the stickle bricks.

Extension ideas

1. Link to topics on ourselves or 'Autumn pictures' (p. 62).
2. Make frames for other pieces of work in the same way using different items to decorate the frames.
3. Collect the twigs for the frames with the children.

Links to Foundation Stage Curriculum

PSE Demonstrate a sense of pride in own achievement (SS)

ELG Select and use activities and resources independently

CLL Use simple statements and questions often linked to gestures (SS)

ELG Interact with others, negotiating plans and activities and taking turns in conversations

KUW Know how to operate simple equipment (SS)

ELG Find out about and identify the uses of everyday technology. Use information and communication technology and programmable toys to support their learning

ACTIVITY 14 # Group of animal pictures

Resources you will need

- Aprons
- Various sized sheets of paper or card
- Shallow containers of paint
- Paintbrushes of various sizes and thicknesses

Aim/concept

- To encourage creative and imaginative skills

Process

- Discuss with the children which animal they are going to paint. It could be a pet or a favourite animal.
- Do they know what colours they need/want?
- Ensure colours that are needed are available or help the children to mix the colours they need.
- Discuss the painting with the children as they paint.
- Offer encouragement throughout.
- When dry, each painting should be mounted on a different coloured sheet of sugar paper or card.
- Hang the individual paintings as part of a group display

Vocabulary/discussion

- Names of animals.
- Discuss features of animals (e.g. tail, whiskers, feet, paws, fins, fur, wool, hide).
- Colours used and shades of colours if mixing colours (e.g. darker, lighter).

Group size

Whole group for discussion then one-to-one for painting

Extension ideas

1. Link to topics on animals.
2. Link to topics on pets.
3. Talk about animals and where you can see them (e.g. in the home, on the farm, or in a zoo or wildlife park).
4. Use small animals to group by feature (e.g. farm animals, has horns).

Links to Foundation Stage Curriculum

PSE	Show confidence in linking up with others for support and guidance (SS)
ELG	Be confident to try new activities, initiate ideas and speak in a familiar group
CLL	Talk activities through, reflecting on and modifying what they are doing (SS)
ELG	Use talk to organise, sequence and clarify thinking, ideas, feelings and events
CD	Use lines to enclose a space, then begin to use these shapes to represent objects (SS)
ELG	Explore colour, shape, form and space in two or three dimensions

ACTIVITY
15 Butterflies

Resources you will need

- Aprons
- Shallow containers of paint, mixed thickly
- Small, chunky paintbrushes or fingers!
- White paper
- Black sugar paper
- Child-sized scissors
- Templates for butterflies
- Pencils

Aim/concept

- To encourage creative skills
- To explore mixing paint colours and noting changes in colour

Process

- Explain the process to the children, showing them the butterfly template and explaining that the butterfly has to be folded when finished.
- Encourage the children to draw around the butterfly templates and cut them out or, provide the children with pre-cut butterflies depending on ability.
- Encourage the children to dab the paint on to the butterflies using either the paintbrushes or fingers, talking about colours of paint.
- When the children have finished, the butterflies need to be folded in half and lightly pressed to transfer the colours on to both sides of the paper. Assist and support as necessary.
- When the butterflies have dried, mount them on to black sugar paper to provide a contrast. Allow a small border and cut to the butterfly shape.
- Encourage the children to write their own name, or write it for them, and mount in the same way as the butterflies alongside them on the display board.

Vocabulary/discussion

- Discuss colours and how paint will be applied, using new descriptive words (e.g. dab, spread, pat)
- Talk about how the colours will be transferred when folded
- Talk about any colours that have been mixed and the results of this
- Introduce comparative language (e.g. the same as, similar, compare)

Group size

4

Links to Foundation Stage Curriculum

PSE Have a strong exploratory impulse (SS)

ELG Continue to be interested, excited and motivated to learn

KUW Talk about what is seen and what is happening (SS)

ELG Look closely at similarities, differences, patterns and changes

Extension ideas

1 Link to topic on growing ('Patch plants a seed' on p.68).
2 Link to topic on mini-beasts.
3 Butterflies can be made without paint. Use scraps of material instead.
4 Butterflies can be displayed in the form of a mobile.

ACTIVITY

16 Salad spinners

Resources you will need

- Coloured paper to mount finished paintings
- Salad spinner
- Paint
- Pipette
- White paper

Salad spinner

Aim/concept

- To explore paint using a salad spinner
- To develop the use of simple tools

Process

- Explain the activity to the children, describing the process of dropping paint into the salad spinner. Explain to the children that they are going to place their circles of paper into the salad spinner, start the salad spinner moving and carefully let drops of paint fall into the moving spinner. Once the spinner has stopped moving they can carefully remove the paper and see the results.
- Encourage the children to cut circles from the white paper, ensuring the circles are the same size as the salad spinner. Explain to the children that the paper has to be the same size, not bigger or smaller.
- Place the paper into the spinner.
- Using a pipette, place drops of paint into the spinner when spinning.
- Experiment with different amounts of paint and when you drop the paint into the spinner look at the different results.

Vocabulary/discussion

- Talk about the results of the process, and the shapes and patterns created by the paint.
- Are there any similarities in the patterns, the colours and the effect of mixing colours?

Group size

6–8

Salad spinner patterns

Extension ideas

1. Link to a topic on spinning (e.g. spinning-tops, fairgrounds, park roundabouts, physical play).
2. Make coloured spinners and twist fast to observe colours changing to 'white'.
3. Make pin wheels and spin plastic plates.
4. Use kaleidescopes.

Links to Foundation Stage Curriculum

MD   Observe and use positional language (SS)

ELG   Use everyday words to describe position

KUW   Show an interest in why things happen and how things work (SS)

ELG   Look closely at similarities, differences, patterns and changes

PD   Engage in activities requiring hand–eye co-ordination (SS)

ELG   Handle tools, objects, construction and malleable materials safely and with increasing control

ACTIVITY 17 Life-sized portraits

Resources you will need

- Rolls of lining paper
- Skin tone paper
- Pens
- Scraps of material
- Balls of wool
- Cartons of various sizes
- Scissors
- PVA glue
- Spreaders

Aim/concept

- To produce life-sized self-portraits

Process

- Talk to the children and explain that you are going to draw around them and cut out the figure for them to 'dress'.
- Explore the resources you have available and allow the children to choose what they would like to use.
- Draw around the child.
- Cut out the figure.
- Place the figure on the floor and allow the children to experiment with the materials they have.
- Discuss whether they would like trousers, skirts, dress, shorts, sari.
- Encourage the children to cut the material to size, measuring as they go.
- Place the fabric and other resources in place and allow the children to make any changes they choose.
- Encourage the children to draw their facial expressions on the paper.
- When the children are finished, help them to glue the items into place.
- Encourage the children to write their own names on labels or write them for them if necessary.
- When dry, display the figures together.

Vocabulary/discussion

- Discuss features and body parts (e.g. eyes, nose, arms, legs, hands)
- Explore fabrics and resources available, and talk about colours, textures
- Introduce positional language (e.g. top, bottom, middle)
- Introduce language to describe size (e.g. smaller, bigger, longer, shorter, taller)

Group size

2–3

Extension ideas

1. Link to topic on ourselves.
2. Link to topics on art.
3. Provide the children with small safety mirrors and encourage them to paint self-portraits.
4. Encourage the children to paint portraits of their friends or family.

Links to Foundation Stage Curriculum

PSE Show willingness to tackle problems and enjoy self-chosen challenges (SS)

ELG Select and use activities and resources independently

PD Engage in activities requiring hand–eye coordination (SS)

ELG Handle tools, objects, construction and malleable materials safely and with increasing control

CD Use their bodies to explore texture and space (SS)

ELG Explore colour, texture, shape, form and space in two or three dimensions

ACTIVITY
18 Autumn pictures

Resources you will need

- Aprons
- Shallow containers of autumn-coloured paints
- Shallow trays for colours to be mixed in
- Brushes
- White paper
- Sugar paper

Aim/concept

- To explore colours and discover what happens when colours are mixed

Process

- Talk to the children about the colours available.
- Ask if the children have seen the colours in their environment. What do the colours remind them of?
- Talk about autumn, focusing particularly on the colours and how they change.
- Explain that they can explore the colours, use them as they are or mix them to make darker or lighter shades.
- Encourage the children to experiment with the colours and to make pictures of whatever they choose, offering help when needed and discussing what they are doing.
- When the paintings have dried, mount them on sugar paper and place on display board.

Vocabulary/discussion

- This activity is about the children exploring the paint and experimenting with colour mixing.
- Discuss the colours, shades, lighter, darker, mixing.
- Talk about where the children may have seen the colours. Have they walked through crunchy leaves? What noises did they make? When do the leaves on the trees change colour? Is it hot or cold when it happens?
- Lots to discuss!

Group size

Whole group for discussion, then pairs for the art work allowing time for further discussion

Matthew C.

Extension ideas

1. Nature walk to look at the colours in the natural environment in the surrounding area.
2. Link to topics on seasons.
3. Discuss with the children the seasons and what happens to trees in each of the seasons.
4. Link to topic on 'Colour display' (p.32).
5. Look at primary colours and carry out activities to mix them and create new colours.

Links to Foundation Stage Curriculum

PSE	Show curiosity (SS)
ELG	Continue to be interested, excited and motivated to learn
CLL	Build up vocabulary that reflects the breadth of their experiences (SS)
ELG	Extend their vocabulary, exploring the meanings and sounds of new words
KUW	Talk about what is seen and what is happening (SS)
ELG	Look closely at similarities, differences, patterns and changes
CD	Begin to differentiate colours (SS)
ELG	Explore colour, texture, shape, form and space in two or three dimensions

ACTIVITY 19 The wheels on the bus

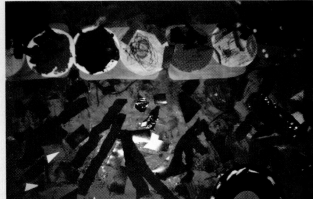

Resources you will need

- Aprons
- Grey paper
- Black paper
- Pencils
- Red glitter
- White paint
- Sponges
- PVA glue
- Brushes
- Felt pens
- Staple gun
- Tissue paper, wool
- Large red paper for the bus
- Circles in 'people paper' colours or paper plates
- Large round shape for the children to use as a template for the wheels
- Scraps of red paper and cellophane
- Shallow trays of skin tone paints
- Child-sized scissors

Aim/concept

- To create a representation of a favourite rhyme, working as part of a group

Process

- Cut out a large bus shape from the red paper.
- Cut windows in the grey paper, making sure there are enough windows to display all the faces, and for a double-decker if necessary.
- Provide the children with paper circles and pencils, and help them draw around the shape and cut them out for the wheels.
- Let the children choose their faces from the colours available, talking about the different colours.
- Encourage the children to paint or draw their faces, allowing them to choose how they do it. Talk about the features with them; what colour eyes do they have? Will their ears show, or will their hair cover them?
- Let the children choose how to create the hair: tissue paper, paint, wool, what do they prefer?
- Lay the bus shape on the floor and encourage the children to place the wheels and windows where they would like them to go. Provide them with PVA glue to fix them in place.
- Encourage the children to cover the rest of the bus in lots of the red resources they have available to them.
- When all the items are dry, encourage the children to choose their windows, where would they like to sit. Talk about bus outings they may have had. Has anyone been on the top of a double-decker bus? What did they see, what was it like?
- Put the display together using a staple gun to fix securely.
- The display shown was produced in the winter months, so the children chose to add snow using sponge blocks in white paint for added effect.

Vocabulary/discussion

- Sing the song 'The wheels on the bus' with the children, talk about the different people and things that are on the bus (e.g. babies crying, bell ringing, wipers swishing).
- Talk about the different parts of the bus (e.g. wheels, windows, and roof).
- Introduce positional language (e.g. top, bottom, middle, back, front).
- Encourage the children to talk about their experiences of buses and to share these with the group.

Group size

6 at a time but try to include all the children in some part of the display other than just making faces. The children also made the border for the display board with sponge shapes and red paint

The wheels on the bus.

Links to Foundation Stage Curriculum

PSE	Demonstrate a sense of pride in own achievement (SS)
ELG	Select and use activities and resources independently
MD	Observe and use positional language (SS)
ELG	Use everyday words to describe position

Extension ideas

1. Link to general topics on stories and rhymes, or transport.
2. Talk in detail about the children's experiences of bus journeys: where did they go?
3. Set up a bus station in the role-play area, providing them with tickets and timetables, and encourage them to go on a bus journey acting out their experiences.

ACTIVITY

20 Patch bakes a cake

Resources you will need

- Empty flour packet
- Empty sugar packet
- Egg box
- Sugar paper in various colours
- 'Patch bakes a cake' by Jo Lodge (Colour Library Direct)
- Margarine lid
- Wooden spoon

- Scissors
- PVA glue
- Pencils
- Blu-tack

Aim/concept

- To re-create the pattern of a story in pictures

Process

- Read the story 'Patch bakes a cake' to the children before the activity so that the narrative is familiar to them.
- Discuss the story with the children in depth and talk about the stages of the story. What did Patch use to make the cake? What did he do with the ingredients next? When the ingredients were mixed, what happened next? When it was cooked, what did it look like?
- Plan with the children what the display will look like. Make a design with them of the pictures.
- Divide the display board into four sections.
- For the first section, the children will need the empty sugar and flour packets and margarine lid and to cut out some eggs to go in the egg box. All the items may be fixed to the display board.
- For the second section, encourage the children to cut out a large mixing bowl from the sugar paper, with a small oval for the top of the bowl. Talk to the children about mixing the ingredients. Attach a wooden spoon to the display board using Blu-tack.
- For the third section, provide the children with a large rectangle of sugar paper for the oven. Talk to the children about the oven door, the handle, the dials and their shapes. Cut out a rectangle for the door and circles for the handle and dials. Provide the children with a round item as a template for the circles and encourage them to cut these out. Help the children to put the oven together using PVA glue and attach the oven to the display board when dry.
- The fourth section is the finished cake. Talk to the children about the cake. What colour would they like? What colour filling? Would they like a different coloured icing on top? How many candles do they need? Help the children make their choices and provide help if needed for drawing and cutting out the shapes.
- Put the cake together using PVA glue and allow to dry.
- When the display is on the board talk to the children about the story again and discuss the order of the sections. Provide the children with the numbers 1 to 4 and place them in the appropriate sections of the board.
- Read the story again and see if the children can match their pictures on the display board to the story.

Vocabulary/discussion

- Talk about the story and relate this to the children's own experiences of making cakes and birthday cakes.
- Discuss the ingredients: do they have these in their cupboards at home? Have they seen the items in the shops?
- Talk about the process of making cakes, change of state when the cake is cooked, and the end-product.
- Do they like cakes? What is their favourite? Do they have cakes for celebrations other than birthdays?

Group size

Whole group for discussion, then smaller groups for the artwork

Extension ideas

1. Make a cake.
2. Link to topics on changes.
3. Link to topics on stories.

Links to Foundation Stage Curriculum

CLL	Use simple statements and questions often linked to gestures (SS)
ELG	Interact with others, negotiating plans and activities and taking turns in conversation
MD	Observe and use positional language (SS)
ELG	Use everyday words to describe position
KUW	Show an interest in why things happen and how things work (SS)
ELG	Ask questions about why things happen and how things work
CD	Make three-dimensional structures (SS)
ELG	Explore colour, texture, shape, form and space in two or three dimensions

ACTIVITY 21 Patch plants a seed

Resources you will need

- Green paper
- Packet of flower seeds
- Beige paper for the flowerpot
- Paper in various colours for the flowers
- 'Patch grows flowers' by Jo Lodge (Colour Library Direct)
- Child's plastic watering can
- Child-sized scissors
- Pictures of flowers
- Blu-tack

Aim/concept

- To re-create the story of 'Patch plants a seed' in a storyboard

Process

- Read the story 'Patch grows flowers'. When you have read the story encourage the children to discuss what happened. What did Patch do first? Did he add anything to the seed and the soil? What did he use? What happened next? Did the plant grow any bigger? Then what? What colour flowers do the children like? Ask them which parts of the story they want to re-create. From this point you can divide the board into number of sections required.
- Plan the display with the children and help them draw a design of the pictures.
- Divide the display into five sections.
- For the first section encourage the children to draw and cut out a flowerpot. Attach this to the wall with a packet of flower seeds. Help the children to cut out tiny pieces of paper for the seeds.
- For the second section you will need another flowerpot and some water. Talk to the children about how all plants need water to grow. Attach the flowerpot and water drops to the board and use Blu-tack to attach the plastic watering can.
- For the third section you will need another flowerpot. Encourage the children to draw and cut out the green shoots of the flower. Talk to the children about the first shoots of the plant. Have they ever grown plants at home?
- For the fourth section you will need a larger version of the flower's shoot with a small bud just breaking out. Encourage the children to draw the parts of the shoot and cut them out. Offer help where needed.
- For the final section you will need another, larger flowerpot. Encourage the children to draw and cut out their own flowers for the display. Talk to the children about their favourite flower or colour, and support them in drawing and cutting them out.
- Put the display together and finish off by numbering the sections. Talk to the children about the display they have created and read the story again.

Vocabulary/discussion

- Encourage the children to talk about the story, the process of planting the seed in soil, watering the seed, watching the first shoot, the buds, the flowers and their colours.
- Do they have flowers in their garden? Have they planted flowers or vegetables in their gardens or windows?
- Encourage them to share their experiences with each other.

Group size

Whole group for discussion, then small groups or pairs.

Extension ideas

1. Link to a topic on growing.
2. Link to a topic on changes.
3. Plant cress seeds in cotton wool and watch them grow, encouraging the children to water them and look after them.
4. Plant seeds and record their growth in pictures, making up booklets.

Links to Foundation Stage Curriculum

CLL	Listen to stories with increasing attention and recall (SS)
ELG	Listen with enjoyment, and respond to stories, songs and other music, rhymes and poems and make up their own stories, songs, rhymes and poems
MD	Show an interest in numbers and counting (SS)
ELG	Recognise numerals 1 to 9
KUW	Show curiosity, observe and manipulate objects (SS)
ELG	Find out about, and identify, some features of living things, objects and events they observe

ACTIVITY 22 Washing line colours

Resources you will need

- Aprons
- White cotton fabric cut into basic clothes shapes
- Small containers of food colouring in various colours
- Elastic bands
- String for the washing line
- Small pegs

Colourful coats

Aim/concept

- To explore the art of tie-dye, discovering wonderful patterns

Process

- Talk to the children and explain the process they are going to follow.
- Let each child choose their own coat to decorate.
- Demonstrate how you wrap the elastic bands around parts of the fabric and help the children do the same.
- Dip small parts of the fabric into the different food colourings.
- Allow the clothes to dry fully. Probably overnight is best.
- Help the children unwrap the elastic bands and discover the patterns they have created.
- For best effect iron the clothes.
- Attach the string to a window frame to create the washing line.
- Help the children hang their clothes on the line with the pegs.

Vocabulary/discussion

- Discuss with the children the patterns they have created, the effect the elastic bands had and the various food colourings

Group size
2–3

Links to Foundation Stage Curriculum

KUW Explore objects (SS)
ELG Ask questions about why things happen and how things work
CD Show an interest in what they see, hear, smell, touch and feel
ELG Respond in a variety of ways to what they see, hear, smell, touch and feel

Extension ideas

1. Marbling painting. This gives a similar effect.
2. Marbled eggs (See *Food and Cooking*, p. 32).
3. Use larger shapes and different fabrics.

ACTIVITY 23 Snowy trees window display

Resources you will need

- White paint mixed with a small amount of washing-up liquid
- Green sugar paper
- Scraps of white and green paper
- Child-sized scissors
- Glue sticks
- Blu-tack

Aim/concept

- To decorate trees for a purpose

Process

- Provide the children with pre-drawn trees on the green sugar paper.
- Encourage the children to cut the shapes out themselves, offering help if required.
- Provide the children with the white and green paper and encourage them to cut pieces to use to decorate their trees. Explain that the trees will be seen from outside as well so it would be good to decorate both sides.
- Ask the children if they would like to add paint to their trees for 'snow'. Encourage them to discuss their own experiences of snow. Have they seen snow before? What did it feel like? Was it warm or cold?
- When the children are happy with their trees help them fix them to the windows, using Blu-tack if it is safe for them to do so. If not, let them direct the adult to their chosen place.
- When the trees are on the windows help the children to paint the snow onto the windows using a sponge and fingertips for the snow flakes. Again, if it is not safe for the children to do this let them direct the adult.

Vocabulary/discussion

- Talk about the children's experiences of snow and encourage them to share their thoughts with the group.
- Have they seen snow? If they have was there lots? Did they make a snowman or go sledging? What clothes did they wear (e.g. gloves, mittens, hats, scarves)?

Group size

6–8

Links to Foundation Stage Curriculum

KUW Remember and talk about significant things that have happened to them

ELG Find out about past and present events in their own lives, and in those of their families and other people they know

CD Pretend that one object represents another, especially when objects have characteristics in common (SS)

ELG Use their imagination in art and design, music, dance, imaginative and role play and stories

Extension ideas

1. Link to topics on weather.
2. Link to topics on seasons.
3. This idea makes an effective card. Use dark blue or black card for added effect.
4. If children are unable to fix trees to windows help them to re-create the same effect on card or sugar paper to produce an effective picture.
5. Make 'snow' by part freezing water and then crushing it up. Watch it melt. How long does this take?

ACTIVITY
24 Incy Wincy Spider

Resources you will need

- Black paper
- Grey paper
- Yellow paper
- Wool
- Child-sized scissors
- Staple gun

Incy Wincy Spider climbed up the water spout,
Down came the rain and washed the spider out.
Out came the sunshine and dried up all the rain.
And Incy Wincy Spider climbed up the spout again.

Aim/concept

- To re-create the pattern of a rhyme in pictures

Process

- Sing the rhyme 'Incy Wincy Spider' with the children, making the actions as they sing. Ensure the children are familiar with the rhyme before the activity.
- Discuss with the children the rhyme in depth, together with the various sections of the rhyme. What happened when it rained? The sun came out. What happened to the rain? What did Incy Wincy Spider do next?
- Discuss the display with the children. Tell them there will be four sections and what do they feel should be in each section? Encourage them to make a plan of the display with your help.
- Divide the board into four sections.
- Split the children into four groups and explain that they are going to complete one section each.
- For the first section the children need to draw and cut out a spider and drainpipe. Talk about the spider: How many legs does he need? What are drainpipes for? Can you see any from your setting? Encourage the children and assist if needed.
- For the second section talk to the children about what happens when it rains. Talk about the rain, raindrops and puddles and clouds. Have they played in puddles? Was it fun? What did they wear?
- For the third section the picture of a sun is required. Encourage the children to draw a large circle and lots of sun rays. If the children are unable to cut the strips for the sun rays, torn paper looks very effective instead.
- For the final section another spider and drainpipe are required as above.
- Once the four sections are ready the adult needs to make a spider's web on the board in section one and four using wool and a staple gun. Talk to the children as you complete this. Have the children seen a spider's web? Where did they see it? What is it for? If possible, take the children outside and see if you can find a web.
- When the display is complete sing the rhyme again with the children and follow the sections on the board as you sing.

Vocabulary/discussion

- Talk to the children about the rhyme and discuss the stages of the rhyme
- Have they seen spiders or webs? Where did they see them?
- Talk about the spiders spinning their webs.

Group size

Whole group for initial discussion, break into small groups of 5–6 for group work, then back to whole group

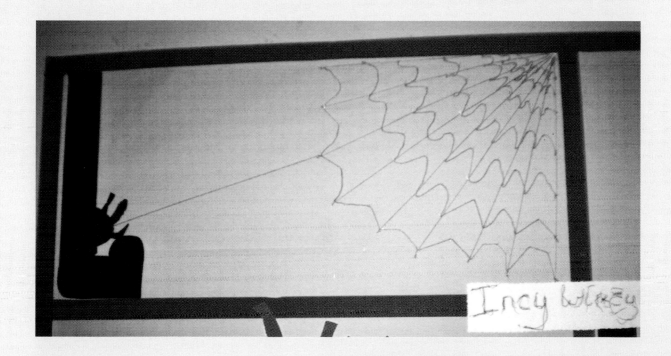

Extension ideas

1. Link to topics on stories and rhymes.
2. Link to topic on mini-beasts.
3. Try to collect spider's webs. Mist them with hairspray and gently dust with talcum powder and transfer to black paper.

Links to Foundation Stage Curriculum

CLL Listen to favourite nursery rhymes, stories and songs. Join in with repeated refrains, anticipating key events and important phrases (SS)

ELG Listen with enjoyment, and respond to stories, songs and other music, rhymes and poems and make up their own stories, songs, rhymes and poems

Photocopiable sheets

Top tips for displays

- Treat every piece of work from a child as a masterpiece.

- Ensure every piece of paper that is given to the children to work on has neat edges.

- Allow the children as much freedom as possible with choice of materials, colours and so on.

- Encourage the children to explore with fabrics, colours and textures.

- Try not to take over a child's work; you may know their idea will not work but let them try.

- Offer support when needed.

- Mount all work carefully.

- Show the children you are proud of their work and let them know they should be proud too.

- Take time to prepare display boards carefully, making sure borders and edges of displays are neat and tidy.

- Point out and discuss the displays with parents and carers, explaining the child's involvement.

- Praise the children for their efforts.

- Enjoy the process and the end-product!

Tips for parents/carers about their children's displays

- Take notice of all displays in your child's nursery/group/class.

- Talk to the staff in your child's setting, find out what the current topics are and what is planned for the near future. Try and extend your child's experiences linked to the topics at home. If the topic is on autumn, try and take a walk in 'crunchy' leaves , point out the trees in the park or find books in the library containing pictures of autumn. Children love to share their experiences with others.

- Most settings will be happy to share their plans with you. You may find you have items connected to the topic that you may be willing to share with the setting. A topic on holidays, for example, photos of past holidays or items from different parts of the country or other countries would be great to share with the children.

- Ask your child about the displays: Can they tell you what they did? What did they do first? Talk about the colours they used. How did they make that pattern?

- Most important is to show your child you are interested and proud of what they have achieved. Lots of praise!

Useful resource suppliers and websites

Consortium 0845 330 7780 www.theconsortium.co.uk

Edprint 01952 248623 www.edprint.co.uk (an excellent source for display backgrounds ready printed)

Galt Educational 08451 203005 www.galt-educational.co.uk

Nursery Education 01926 887799 www.scholastic.co.uk

Nursery World 020 7782 3000 www.nurseryworld.co.uk

Scrapstore www.childrenscrapstore.co.uk (use the directory for local suppliers)

Step by step 08451 252550 www.sbs-educational.co.uk

S&S Services 01789 765323 www.ss-services.co.uk

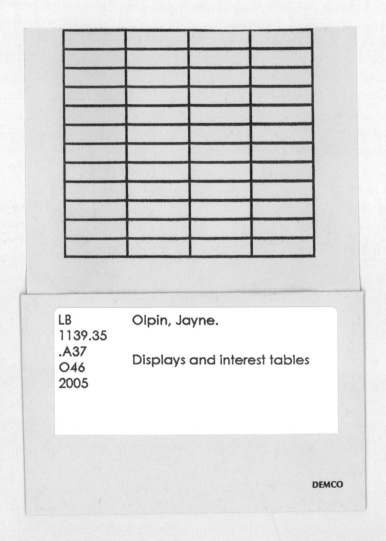